American Symbols

The White House

By Lloyd G. Douglas

Welcome Books™

Children's Press®
A Division of Scholastic Inc.
New York / Toronto / London / Auckland / Sydney
Mexico City / New Delhi / Hong Kong
Danbury, Connecticut

Photo Credits: Cover © EyeWire, Inc.; pp. 5, 13 © Corbis; p. 7 © Alan Schein Photography/Corbis; p. 9 © Wally McNamee/Corbis; pp. 11, 19 © Bettmann/Corbis; pp. 15, 17 © AP/Wide World Photos p. 21 © Lester Lefkowitz/Corbis
Contributing Editor: Jennifer Silate
Book Design: Christopher Logan

Library of Congress Cataloging-in-Publication Data

Douglas, Lloyd G.
    The White House / by Lloyd G. Douglas.
    p. cm.—(American symbols)
    Includes index.
    Summary: Uses easy-to-read text to introduce the White House as an American symbol.
    ISBN 0-516-25855-9 (lib. bdg.)—ISBN 0-516-27878-9 (pbk.)
    1. White House (Washington, D.C.)—Juvenile literature. 2. Presidents—United States—Juvenile literature. 3. Washington (D.C.)—Buildings, structures, etc.—Juvenile literature. [1. White House (Washington, D.C.) 2. Presidents. 3. Washington (D.C.)—Buildings, structures, etc.] I. Title. II. Series: Douglas, Lloyd G. American symbols.

F204.W5 D68 2003
975.3—dc21

2002155451

Contents

The **White House** has been a **symbol** of America for more than two hundred years.

The **president** of the United States lives in the White House with his family.

5

The **address** of the White House is 1600 Pennsylvania Avenue.

It is in Washington, D.C.

PENNSYLVANIA AV NW

1600

7

Many presidents have lived in the White House.

John Adams was the first president to live in the White House.

He was the second president of the United States.

11

The White House has many rooms.

The president works in a room called the **Oval Office**.

The East Room is the largest room in the White House.

Many parties and dinners have been held there.

15

People can visit some parts of the White House.

Many people visit the White House every year.

On the Monday after Easter, many children go to the White House.

They roll **Easter eggs** on the front lawn.

19

The White House is the most **famous** home in America.

It is an important American symbol.

New Words

address (uh-**dress**) the street and town where something is

Easter eggs (**ee**-stur **egz**) decorated eggs for Easter

famous (**fay**-muhs) known by many people

Oval Office (**oh**-vuhl **awf**-is) the room where the president works, it is shaped like an egg

president (**prez**-uh-duhnt) the leader of a country or a group of people

symbol (**sim**-buhl) a drawing or an object that stands for something else

White House (**wite houss**) the place where the president of the United States of America lives

To Find Out More

Books
The Story of the White House
by Kate Waters
Scholastic Inc.

The White House
by Lynda Sorensen
The Rourke Book Company

Web Site
White House Kids
http://www.whitehouse.gov/kids
Learn about the White House and all the people and
animals that live there.

Index

About the Author
Lloyd G. Douglas is an editor and writer of children's books.

Reading Consultants

Kris Flynn, Coordinator, Small School District Literacy, The San Diego County Office of Education

Shelly Forys, Certified Reading Recovery Specialist, W.J. Zahnow Elementary School, Waterloo, IL

Sue McAdams, Former President of the North Texas Reading Council of the IRA, and Early Literacy Consultant, Dallas, TX